First World War
and Army of Occupation
War Diary
France, Belgium and Germany

2 DIVISION
6 Infantry Brigade
King's (Liverpool Regiment)
7th Battalion
1 March 1915 - 31 December 1915

WO95/1360/2

The Naval & Military Press Ltd
www.nmarchive.com
Published in association with The National Archives

Published by

The Naval & Military Press Ltd

Unit 10 Ridgewood Industrial Park,

Uckfield, East Sussex,

TN22 5QE England

Tel: +44 (0) 1825 749494

www.naval-military-press.com

www.nmarchive.com

This diary has been reprinted in facsimile from the original. Any imperfections are inevitably reproduced and the quality may fall short of modern type and cartographic standards.

© Crown Copyright
Images reproduced by permission of The National Archives, London, England, 2015.

Contents

Document type	Place/Title	Date From	Date To
Heading	WO95/1360/2		
Heading	2 Div 6 Brigade 1/7 Bn Kings Liver Pool 1915 Mar-1915 Dec		
Heading	2nd Division War Diaries 7th Battn Kings Liverpool Regt. From 1st March To 30 April 1915		
Heading	2nd Division 6th Brigade War Diary 7th Battalion Kings" Liverpool Regiment March 1915		
War Diary	Canterbury	01/03/1915	07/03/1915
War Diary	Allouagne	10/03/1915	11/03/1915
War Diary	Vendin Les Bathunes	12/03/1915	19/03/1915
War Diary	Bethune	20/03/1915	26/03/1915
War Diary	Annequin	27/03/1915	31/03/1915
Heading	2nd Division 6th Brigade. War Diary 7th Battalion King's Liverpool Regiment April 1915		
War Diary	Annequin	01/04/1915	10/04/1915
War Diary	Bethune	11/04/1915	14/04/1915
War Diary	Annequin	17/04/1915	20/04/1915
War Diary	Bethune	21/04/1915	24/04/1915
War Diary	Annequin	25/04/1915	28/04/1915
War Diary	Bethune	29/04/1915	30/04/1915
Heading	2nd Division War Diaries 1/7th Battn. Kings Liverpool Regt. From 1st May. To 31st August 1915		
Heading	6th Infantry Brigade. 2nd Division War Diary 1/7th Battn. The King's (LIverpool) Regiment. May 1915		
War Diary	Bethune	01/05/1915	08/05/1915
War Diary	Le Conture	09/05/1915	09/05/1915
War Diary	Richebourg St Vaast Le Touret	10/05/1915	13/05/1915
War Diary	Rue des Charattes	14/05/1915	15/05/1915
War Diary	Line A	16/05/1915	17/05/1915
War Diary	German Front Second Line	18/05/1915	19/05/1915
War Diary	Le Conture	20/05/1915	20/05/1915
War Diary	Allauagne	21/05/1915	29/05/1915
War Diary	Les Brebis	30/05/1915	31/05/1915
Heading	Notes on Holding "W" Section.		
Miscellaneous	Notes on Holding "W" Section.		
Heading	6th Infantry Brigade. 2nd Division War Diary 1/7th Battn. The King's (Liverpool) Regiment. June 1915		
War Diary	Les Brebis	01/06/1915	04/06/1915
War Diary	Marroc	05/06/1915	06/06/1915
War Diary	Noeux-Les-Mines	07/06/1915	07/06/1915
War Diary	Noyelles-Les-Vermelles	08/06/1915	14/06/1915
War Diary	Vaudricourt	15/06/1915	19/06/1915
War Diary	Cuinchy	20/06/1915	22/06/1915
War Diary	Annequin	23/06/1915	26/06/1915
War Diary	Cuinchy	27/06/1915	30/06/1915
Heading	6th Infantry Brigade. 2nd Division War Diary 1/7th Battn. The King's (Liverpool) Regiment. July 1915		
War Diary	Tourbieres	01/07/1915	05/07/1915
War Diary	Vendin	06/07/1915	12/07/1915
War Diary	Vendin Givenchy	13/07/1915	13/07/1915

War Diary	Givenchy	14/07/1915	16/07/1915
War Diary	Bethune	17/07/1915	20/07/1915
War Diary	Givenchy	21/07/1915	24/07/1915
War Diary	Le Preol	25/07/1915	27/07/1915
War Diary	Vendin	28/07/1915	31/07/1915
Heading	6th Infantry Brigade 2nd Division War Diary 1/7th Battn. The King's (Liverpool) Regiment. August 1915		
War Diary	Vendin-Lez-Bethune	01/08/1915	02/08/1915
War Diary	Essars	03/08/1915	28/08/1915
War Diary	Bivouac	29/08/1915	31/08/1915
Heading	2nd Division 5th Infy Bde 1-7th Battalion The King's (Liverpool Regt) Sep-Nov 1915		
Heading	5th Infantry Brigade. 2nd Division War Diary 1/7th Battn. The King's (Liverpool Regiment). September 1915		
War Diary	Bivouacs	01/09/1915	02/09/1915
War Diary	Essars	03/09/1915	23/09/1915
War Diary	Trenches	24/09/1915	24/09/1915
War Diary	Trenches Essars	25/09/1915	25/09/1915
War Diary	Essars	26/09/1915	26/09/1915
War Diary	Essars Trenches	27/09/1915	28/09/1915
War Diary	Essars	29/09/1915	30/09/1915
Heading	5th Infantry Brigade 2nd Division War Diary 1/7th Battn. The King's (Liverpool Regiment). October 1915		
War Diary	Essars Vermelles	01/10/1915	02/10/1915
War Diary	Bethune	03/10/1915	04/10/1915
War Diary	Essars	06/10/1915	09/10/1915
War Diary	Annequin	10/10/1915	21/10/1915
War Diary	Annezin	21/10/1915	28/10/1915
War Diary	Beuvry	29/10/1915	31/10/1915
Heading	5th Infantry Brigade 2nd Division War Diary 1/7th Battn. The King's (Liverpool Regiment). November 1915		
War Diary	Beuvry	01/11/1915	04/11/1915
War Diary	Bethune	05/11/1915	10/11/1915
War Diary	Le Preol	11/11/1915	11/11/1915
War Diary	Bethune	12/11/1915	12/11/1915
War Diary	Trenches	13/11/1915	13/11/1915
War Diary	Bethune Trenches	14/11/1915	21/11/1915
War Diary	Bethune	22/11/1915	25/11/1915
War Diary	Lechoquaux	26/11/1915	27/11/1915
War Diary	Bethune	28/11/1915	30/11/1915
Heading	War Diary 22nd Inf. Bde. 1/7 Battn, The King's Regiment (the Liverpools) Dec., 1915		
Heading	1/7 Bn. Liverpools Rg. Dec Vol IX		
War Diary	Bethune	01/12/1915	04/12/1915
War Diary	Fontes-St-Hilaire	05/12/1915	05/12/1915
War Diary	Briquemesnil	06/12/1915	28/12/1915
War Diary	Warlus	29/12/1915	31/12/1915

WO95 1360 (2)

2 DIN

6 BRIGADE

1/7 BN KINGS LIVERPOOL

1915 MAR - 1915 DEC

JOSSON   165 BDE

2nd Division

War Diaries

7th Battn Kings Liverpool Regt.

From 1st March, To 30 April 1915

2nd Division.
6th Brigade.

Disembarked at Havre from
United Kingdom 8th March 1915.

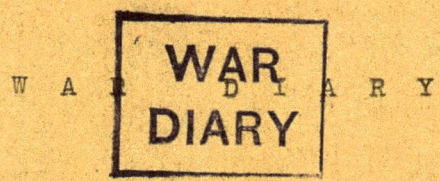

7th Battalion KING'S (LIVERPOOL) REGIMENT

March

1 9 1 5

WAR DIARY or INTELLIGENCE SUMMARY

(Erase heading not required.)

Army Form C. 2118.

Hour, Date, Place	Summary of Events and Information	Remarks and references to Appendices
1915 March 1st Canterbury	Company parades morning & afternoon. Hands in Stores & draws Barrack Furniture. Board on unexpended Rations.	
" 2nd "	Batt'n Route March, accompanied by transport in the morning. Company parade afternoon.	
" 3rd "	Batt'n Route March accompanied by Transport. Company parades in the afternoon.	
" 4th "	20 sent to Canvas. Attack & defence. B'n warned for embarkation on 4/3/15.	
" 5th "	Route March.	
" 6th "	Medical inspection of whole Batt'n. Practicing formations under Artillery fire. Cleared up Camp.	
" 7th "	Batt'n left England for France. Left Canterbury in two trains. Entrainment & detrainment was well carried out. All the train were able to have their afternoon tea before being off train to the train & to the time of embarking at Southampton in two hours & a half. Time Headquarters in SS Duchess of Argyll, 2 officers & 50 other ranks. Rafted a close H.T. 150 men aboard S.S. Mona Queen, Intentry of Batt'n.	
" 8th Havre	Disembarked at 4 am & marched to Rest Camp. Remained at Rest Camp. Men allowed into town on account of their arrival in Camp at 10 Am made a stay absolutely necessary. Batt'n marches of to Entrainment (16 officers entrain'g with B.H.Q. & left @ 9.15 PM. Men going off in other trains). Ent'd Officers Mess arrange	1/8

WAR DIARY
or
INTELLIGENCE SUMMARY.
(Erase heading not required.)

Army Form C. 21

Hour, Date, Place	Summary of Events and Information	Remarks and references to Appendices

1915

June 10th Allonagne

11.15 — Battn reached Calonne about 4pm, after detrains- traint marched to Allonagne. Billets in the Sole Roles difficult, out to movement under the angle of fuller in this end.

20 — Two Platoons arrived in the morning. C.O. & A.S.T. went to report at front office testing handed by Sgt Cunip. Sent back & marched in the afternoon to Camp.

10th Vendin les Béthune

13.15 SO — The Battn marched Tuesday in the morning accompanied Transport Billets arranged before arrival. (C.O. S.A.T) Battn to be H.Q. A.C. (Battns) after dinner Platoons to be HQ and to town of the and Received orders to stand by for about notice. Drew in readiness Platoons etc. Orders received at 9.35pm. But were not called for till during the night.

14.15 SO — Company training in the morning. Inspection by G.O.C.
15.00 SO — 2nd Divn by G.O.C. on the in the afternoon. Stand by to more at the notice at night - received orders after. (No move of the order to 3 files.

16.15 SO — Church Parade.
17.15 S — Company Parades in the morning and afternoon. To go to Be Same to see the work being carried out. Company Training in the morning. Brigadier General & regiment Came to the S'Iward. Went to see the general. They had dinner 5:35 - Running Dog. Estranges on the Lewonder two enge went to the trenches for two guides. To be companied on two numbered trench. They left about 8:30 led by (2) Res 90 on main Road. They set guides at 6am.

Army Form C. 2118

WAR DIARY
or
INTELLIGENCE SUMMARY.
(Erase heading not required.)

Instructions regarding War Diaries and Intelligence Summaries are contained in F.S. Regs., Part II. and the Staff Manual respectively. Title pages will be prepared in manuscript.

Hour, Date, Place 1915		Summary of Events and Information	Remarks and references to Appendices
Vandon Ro - Bethune	March 15th	Trench drill — Running drill — Rifle Exercises — B & C Coys rested in the morning. Generals Munro, Horne & Fanshawe came to see us in the afternoon. Interviewed the Ex Cmdrs of B & C on the air occurrences. We lost a return football team of 1st & 5th Inver Fuss. 6 - 2 yesterday.	
Do	19th	Batn Route marched — It was bitterly cold. Snow fell in the night & lies 3 ins deep when we were marching. The Baths gave 2 concert in Bethune.	
Bethune	20th		
Do	21st	We got orders to move in the middle of last night but they were countermanded	

Army Form C. 2118.

WAR DIARY
or
INTELLIGENCE SUMMARY.
(Erase heading not required.)

Instructions regarding War Diaries and Intelligence Summaries are contained in F. S. Regs., Part II. and the Staff Manual respectively. Title pages will be prepared in manuscript.

Hour, Date, Place	Summary of Events and Information	Remarks and references to Appendices
Bethune March 25th		
" 26"		
Annequin " 27"		
" 28"		
29th		
" 30th		
" 31st		

2nd Division.
6th Brigade.

Disembarked at Havre from
United Kingdom 8th March 1915.

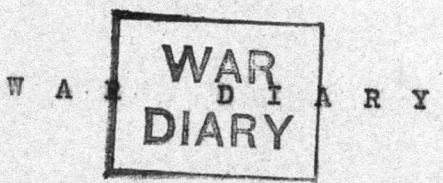

7th Battalion KING'S (LIVERPOOL) REGIMENT

April

1 9 1 5

Instructions regarding War Diaries and Intelligence Summaries are contained in F. S. Regs., Part II. and the Staff Manual respectively. Title pages will be prepared in manuscript.

WAR DIARY
or
INTELLIGENCE SUMMARY.
(Erase heading not required.)

Army Form C. 2118.

1915 Hour, Date, Place	Summary of Events and Information	Remarks and references to Appendices
Annequin April 1st	The possibility of an attack was anticipated. The whole Bde were in the trenches. A Coy marched out from Bethune & arrived about 4-30 am. The remainder of the Batt. less two platoons of 'B' Coy who were already in the trenches moved off at 5 am. There was no attack & we returned at 10-15 am. 'A' Coy remained at Tourbieres so that now the whole Batt. is up.	7/8
Do 2nd	'C' Coy relieved B in the trenches. Several of our officers attended an experiment with the Bangalore torpedo in the afternoon. It was entirely successful in blowing up close & very strongly made entanglements but no use for open entanglements. [A feint attack was carried out during the night & early hours of the morning (secret instructions attached) It commenced after dark with the blowing up of the entanglements & culminated at 5am by blowing up an enemy trench. Both these items were entirely successful	
Do 3rd	Nothing to report. A good bit of shelling by the Germans.	
Do 4th	'D' relieved C in the trenches. 3 casualties all wounded. 'C' Coy tested their rifles in the trenches, none of our rifles could be considered in a tip top condition. There are many jams & miss fires	
Do 5th	'A' Coy tested their rifles in the trenches & drew a considerable amount of shell fire. The Germans shelled more or less all day. We had one man killed.	
Do 6th	A Coy relieved D Coy in the trenches. Owing to 2 platoons not being required in the support trenches a half Coy is now billeted in Annequin. Two casualties to-day. [illegible] at Tourbieres	

Army Form C. 2118

WAR DIARY
or
INTELLIGENCE SUMMARY.
(Erase heading not required.)

Hour, Date, Place	Summary of Events and Information	Remarks and references to Appendices
Annequin April 4th 1915	The Regt were given a lecture by OC and talks also by Two Coys A & B went in to trenches and stretcher party was on CUINCHY Defences. C [Coy] Headqrs also at ANNEQUIN. D in charge of [illegible] for sanitation. We also did [illegible] on CAMBRIN front. One Coy stays for afternoon to the old Coy	
5 [AM]	A & B Company were in trenches on movement. Trenches and musketry ranges	
9 [AM]	C & D Coys medical lecture & fatigues. A & B Coys in trenches. Lectures on hygiene and communication.	We [illegible]
10 [AM]	We use Coys not in the trenches went for afternoon to see [illegible]	CUINCHY was heavily shelled but no casualties
11 [AM]	No events of any importance occurred	
	We were relieved by 5th Inf. Brigade and [illegible] at BETHUNE	Let over 15 30 35th
Bethune April 5th 1915	We went to our billets [illegible]	
	BEAJURY [?] BC Hqrs HQ [illegible] breakfast at 5.30 am to be [illegible] at 7.30 am	Bombardment of the night out at 0.5 [illegible] [illegible] men dressed & paraded
April 5th 1915		

Army Form C. 211

WAR DIARY
or
INTELLIGENCE SUMMARY.
(Erase heading not required.)

Instructions regarding War Diaries and Intelligence Summaries are contained in F.S. Regs., Part II. and the Staff Manual respectively. Title pages will be prepared in manuscript.

Hour, Date, Place	Summary of Events and Information	Remarks and references to Appendices
1915		
Bethune April 13th	The Machine gun section returned to Bn.	One of our bombers
	went into the billets between 1 and 2 am.	slightly
	The mules taken right up to the ration's	
	march were struck.	
	By trenches. Breach Bund Terror.	Clear by Burnt Stores
	By Annequin Bay.	on of German.
" 14th		
" 15th 11am sniping continued.		
Annequin " 16th 2.15pm Marched to the trenches C & D Coys in	A & B Coys in a at Cambrin a Bat Annequin.
	Five men of C wounded, one of A wounded at Cuinchy. Shot at one	
" 17th One man A Coy wounded	A Coy ordered to make an attack German
" 18th C Coy 2 all quiet	The trenches. Made a C Coy heavy to return to
" 19th relieved by Scott went in to Coy. Heavy fire from the
" 20th Cuinchy trenches.	About 10 casualties German in
	No casualties.	
Beaune " 21st Returned to Beaune. Machine gun section returned.
" 22nd 7. Charges and etc., frame carried in as
" 23rd C & D Coy sent up to trenches.	
" 24th Result unknown first Lt Pilkenright wounded.
" 25th Marched to trenches A & B Coy in a Cambrin & C Annequin.
" 26th That night Sgt Morgan & Dmr McDonald recommend Germans name
Annequin " " enter trenches took about 12 men of Sgt	water & Sgt.
	Crater. Returned to make a left sent at &
	We lost 3 LC's & 14 ORs at 5.30pm uses Lewis A Damo Taylor
" 27th " 1 recruit.	about 25 by crater occupied
		a german line of crater

WAR DIARY or INTELLIGENCE SUMMARY

Army Form C. 2118

Hour, Date, Place	Summary of Events and Information	Remarks and references to Appendices
Armeçain April 31st (cont)	31st May Hodge (A Coy) was started out but was not but serious to get at but fortunately resulted in chaos instead of attack.	
	was successfully accomplished by 3am with no loss of life.	
	6.30 H.M.S. arrived. Lt H Agacanty & Lt Kent R.E.	
	covering meeting at L.K. Adams. May Hodges were in charge of	
	various parties	
	G.O.C. made rest of trenches in & captured entire satisfaction	
25th —	Recieved by 5th Devonshire. Had before two Coys 2.T.D. at Armagin	
24th —	afternoon.	
30th —		
May 1st —	arrived	
2nd —		
3rd —	OC Coys met on accd of Bottomag at	
4th —	Bottomay on accd of	
	tactical at 6.30am	
Bottomay	FARM left at 7am got back at 3pm	Infantry Coffee (?) for O.C.
5th —		

2nd Division

War Diaries

1/11th Battn. Kings Liverpool Regt.

From 1st May. To 31st August 1915

6th Infantry Brigade.
2nd Division.

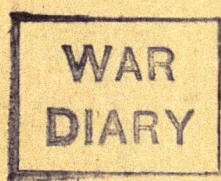

1/7th BATTN. THE KING'S (LIVERPOOL) REGIMENT.

M A Y

1 9 1 5

Attached:

Notes on holding "W" Section.

WAR DIARY or **INTELLIGENCE SUMMARY.**
(Erase heading not required.)

Army Form C. 2118
7/8/17

Hour, Date, Place	Summary of Events and Information	Remarks and references to Appendices
Bethune. May 1st	Coy training morning & afternoon. (5 Suffolk had 2 men killed & 4 wounded in the Church Parade.)	(opp. to Centre)
" 2nd	"	
" 3rd	C.O. & Coys reformed at Bethune & also Machine Gun Sect. C.O. returned from leave.	
" 4th	Battalion practised an assault on enemy's trenches at Vertbois Farm, &c.	
" 5th	Left at 9.30 A.M. & got back about 3.30 P.m. Very hot march.	
" 6th	Coy Parades.	
6th 7th	Coy Parades in morning. Route march in afternoon.	
7th	Coy Parades in morning. Packed & intending to move over night, orders were cancelled later for 2nd May.	
8th	Batt. moved off at 1-3.0 am, joined the Bde. at Gonnehem about 4 am & proceeded on march to Hingette. At 5 am Art. 20 Commencement commenced.	
9th	Batt. was in Reserve for the attack. At 5 pm Batt. moved forward to Bde. dump & waited orders to stand by at 6 pm.	
Le Touret	10.15 St. off to all Coys.	
	11.15 Moved off to reach B. Pot.	
	12.15 Batn training - Bde night operations (Advance to attack across country)	
	13.15 A & B Coys went into the trenches - Remainder of Batn moved to	
Rue des Chavattes	head of Rue des Chavattes	
	14.15 Conference with G.O.C. Bde. - Troops resting. Reconnoitred enemy's lines from Artillery Observation Posts.	

(73989) W4141—463. 400,000. 9/14. H.&J. Ltd. Forms/C. 2118/10.

WAR DIARY of INTELLIGENCE SUMMARY.
(Erase heading not required.)

Army Form C. 2118

7/8/7

Hour, Date, Place	Summary of Events and Information	Remarks and references to Appendices
1915		
Aude des Charottes May 15th	After conference with G.O.C. 1st Bde we attack to-night. The Regt moves into front line during the afternoon. Attack started at 11.30 p.m. A & B Coys in attack. About 10.45 p.m. D Coy wanted. Attack successful, Germans ran. Target carried. H & B took up ammunition later.	
May 16th	Attack continued. Attempted to reach up reinforcements but we were unable to make headway. About 200 or so of our men were numerous. Fine day, 250 men [...] casualties about 9 officers [...] about 220 other ranks wounded. [...] cont. A Bde to leave us to bombardment at different times through the day.	
May 17th	It is suggested to germans behind the latter lines A. Ford a first-gone [...] Scots. Ours is not writing is [...] in German [...] camp at noon & [...] fair casualties. Before moves into German line we were at [...] ourselves to new trench 1st king took over a battn sent to make good. Again under artillery fire some german shells [...] one of our [...] no casualties. A great many german shells were sent over.	
May 18th	About midnight German [...] most of the day. Bolts relieved us & we went to continue.	
May 19th		
May 20th Le Couture	Till about 1-15 p.m. we stop in billets at [...] moved by motor bus for a rest. We moved off at about [...] a half at [...] marched [...] after dinner. It was a hot march. The weather	

WAR DIARY
or
INTELLIGENCE SUMMARY

(Erase heading not required.)

Army Form C. 2118

Instructions regarding War Diaries and Intelligence Summaries are contained in F.S. Regs., Part II. and the Staff Manual respectively. Title pages will be prepared in manuscript.

Hour, Date, Place	Summary of Events and Information	Remarks and references to Appendices
Allouagne May 20th (Cont)	Rec'd orders to move about 5.30pm. Arrived about 8pm. Not over comfortable billets.	In trenches and approaches
May 21st	Troops resting. Fired 3 rifle inspections.	
May 22nd	G.O.C. 3rd Division spoke to Batt'n on parade & complimented us on the recent fighting.	
May 23rd	Church parade.	
May 24th	Batt'n instructions by C.O. Company training in afternoon.	
May 25th	Company training. Grenade throwing.	
May 26th	Route march.	
May 27th	Company training. Practical use of respirators.	
May 28th	Coy Training	
May 29th	Coy Training	
May 30th	Batt'n moved into [?] to take over part of French line, south of La Bassée	
May 31st Les Brebis	Reconnoitred the line. No tramway can be cannot be [?] own its limits. No communication from shell fire & several alterations & much improvements in the [?] the streets.	

(73969) W4141—463. 400,000. 9/14. H.&J.Ltd. Forms/C. 2118/10.

NOTES ON HOLDING "W" SECTION.

Secret. G.S.49

Notes on holding "W" section.

1. There will be three subsections W.1, W.2, W.3, each held by one battalion — Bucks & Rifles W.1, Staffs or 1/Kings W.2, 5th or 7th Liverpools W.3.

2. To ensure that the Brigade is at all times ready to march no platoon or machine gun detachment will be on duty in the firing line of trenches for more than 24 hours at the time.
   Reliefs of Companies and Battalions will be arranged accordingly.

3. To enable the Brigade to assume the offensive at the shortest notice either in the form of a counter attack immediately after the repulse of an enemy's attack or to attack after two hours notice by day or night each subsection will —

   (a) Reconnoitre at once and continue to reconnoitre to ascertain the best line in the enemy's lines opposite the subsection and the best way there by day & night.

   (b) Settle and prepare all arrangements for forming up the infantry of the section to make from the front line the attack on the objective selected and for holding its own line whilst the attack is carried out.

   (c) Arrange where it will get out of its own trenches and the best way to our own line by day or night.

   (d) Arrange the best way of supporting the other subsections on its right or left by fire or by moving its force required to support them in counter attack.

4. In case of attack —

   (a) The front line will be held.

   (b) Should the enemy succeed in penetrating anywhere the subsection commanders will at once counter attack the trenches the front line occupying by bombing down the trenches and by fire from their front to stop the enemy reinforcing. Subsections commanders on the right and left will cooperate in accordance with para 3(d) taking steps to front all counter attacks if the other section Commanders attacked have not been able to rejoin them.

   (c) The artillery will open fire with the enemy breaks the front wire or next covering the trenches in accordance

   going

6th Infantry Brigade.
2nd Division.

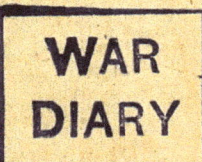

1/7th BATTN. THE KING'S (LIVERPOOL) REGIMENT.

J U N E

1 9 1 5

June 1915

5th Liverpool Regt (T.F.)

WAR DIARY or INTELLIGENCE SUMMARY
Army Form C. 2118

Hour, Date, Place	Summary of Events and Information	Remarks and references to Appendices
June 1st LES BREBIS	Coy paraded. Coy Offr [?] reconnoitred the trenches.	
2nd do	Coy paraded. Coy Offrs Fatg Squad.	
3rd do	Coy paraded. A & B Coys fatg. working parts to trenches.	
4th do	Reduced 5th enters in trenches after 9am.	
5th MARROC	Bde on left bank, Germans were [?] to attack at night. We stood to [?] Wounded French Artillery. Nothing occurred. Fd Coy 900 abandoned. O/C Brock Williams B Oatfield arrived.	
6th do	Arrived at 11pm in LONDON Divn. Marched to Ridlectes [?] Coys to NOEUX-LES-MINES where we were billeted.	
7th NOEUX-LES-MINES	Bde troops were made up in line further North. Marched off South to No 1 at NOYELLES-LES-VERMELLES. 10am [?] last few miles were very misty; which was useful on account of the continuous fire of the troops & [?] No shots were fired or men were [?] out & [?] the enemy.	
8th NOYELLES-LES-VERMELLES	Coy training (Carried on much on account of research, started to be unwary [?] Covery trench [?] Coy offrs. [?] reconnoitred the trenches.	
9th do	Coy training. C & D Coys Fatigue in front of the line at LE RUTOIRE	
10th do	A & B Coys do do	
11th do	do Inspection of bildgs [?] C & D 7:55 Fatigue at LE RUTOIRE	
12th do	Wade Batt. on 7:55 for one at night	
13th do	Church parades. Wade Batt. on 7:55 for one at night	
14th do	Bde relieved by 5th Bde. Marched to billets at VAUDRICOURT at 10	

June 1915 — 4th Divisional Royal Engineers (TF)

Army Form C. 2118.

WAR DIARY or INTELLIGENCE SUMMARY
(Erase heading not required.)

Instructions regarding War Diaries and Intelligence Summaries are contained in F.S. Regs., Part II. and the Staff Manual respectively. Title pages will be prepared in manuscript.

Hour, Date, Place	Summary of Events and Information	Remarks and references to Appendices
June 15th VAUDRICOURT	Coy. Route march. Orders at 6 pm to stand by at 2 hours notice. At 11 pm ordered to 1 hour notice. Orders received at dawn.	
16th 8 am	Coy stand down	
" 3 pm	3.10 men sent for 3/5D at VERMELLES	
" 19th	Working parties returned at 6 am. Orders received to move at 10 am to place ourselves at command of CO 3rd Bde at CUINCHY. Radnor, Page & it.	
" 20th CUINCHY	3rd Bde at CUINCHY relieved by rifle brigade	
" 21st	Smoke shells 13 unexploded.	
" 22nd	Sent 30'	
"	Enemy exploded a mine & made a crater 30c. Br. relieved by Inds. also sent at mine at ANNEQUIN 2/Lts HOLLAND, ROBINSON, STEVENSON,	
23rd ANNEQUIN	Bde to ANNEQUIN	
" 24th & 26th	RUTHERFORD 3 off & 67 OR	
"	Bde. moves. Fell instruction etc	
" 26th	Coy. Photos. Wire pickets for R.E.	
"	Brown shelled. ANNEQUIN & went Great. 1 wounded 2/Lts 8 wounded. Relieved by 6 Bn. stafford brigade from 10th to 10.45	
AUCHY-LA-BASSEE from 10 to 10.45		
" 27th CUINCHY	On Art. Coy. 8 OR 1/2 trenches about 6 am tonight. Enemy exploded a small mine in trenches also countermine & 11th by in our line at 5-30.	
" 28th	We learnt that more mines about to explode gun fire before midnight but nothing & found. Attempt unsuccessful	
" 29th 30	1 Man wounded.	
" 30th	Relieved by 5th Durham/stafford at 1-30. We took over authorities mine at CUINCHY SUPPORT H	
	A Coy MAISON ROUGE, B Coy CAMBRIN, D Coy CUINCHY SUPPORT H	
	C Coy. No. go TOURBIERES	

6th Infantry Brigade.
2nd Division.

1/7th BATTN. THE KING'S (LIVERPOOL) REGIMENT.

J U L Y

1 9 1 5

Sheet 1

Army Form C. 2118.

WAR DIARY
or
INTELLIGENCE SUMMARY.
(Erase heading not required.)

Instructions regarding War Diaries and Intelligence Summaries are contained in F.S. Regs., Part II. and the Staff Manual respectively. Title pages will be prepared in manuscript.

Place	Hour, Date	Summary of Events and Information	Remarks and references to Appendices
TOURBIÈRES	July 2nd	One Company in trenches at CUINCHY SUPPORT POINT; one at CAMBRIN SUPPORT POINT, remaining two at TOURBIÈRES.	W.R.
do	" 3rd	do	W.R.
do	" 4th	do	W.R.
do	" 4th	TOURBIÈRES shelled 8 to 10 am. Shew burnt down. Headquarters moved. 9 killed, 19 wounded.	W.R.
do	" 5th	Moved to VENDIN arriving about 9 pm.	W.R.
VENDIN	" 6th	Company training (& refitting) till 12.30	W.R.
VENDIN	" 7th	Running drill 7 am Coy training 9.30 am.	W.R.
do	" 8th	Battalion formed front of guard of honour to F.M. Earl Kitchener	W.R.
do	" 9th	Daily training	W.R.
do	" 10th	do	W.R.
do	" 11th	do Church Parade	W.R.
do	" 12th	Daily training	W.R.

a/ K.R. Rutherford. Lieut.
ADJT. 7TH BN THE KING'S (L'POOL) REGT.

Sheet D

WAR DIARY
or
INTELLIGENCE SUMMARY.
(Erase heading not required.)

Army Form C. 2118

Instructions regarding War Diaries and Intelligence Summaries are contained in F.S. Regs., Part II. and the Staff Manual respectively. Title pages will be prepared in manuscript.

Hour, Date, Place		Summary of Events and Information	Remarks and references to Appendices
RENDIN GIVENCHY	July 13th	The Battalion took over B.1. sector of trenches at GIVENCHY. Relief complete 3.30 p.m. A & B Companies in front line. C & D in support	W.R.
GIVENCHY	July 14th	Weather very bad	W.R.
do	" 15th	Trenches.	W.R.
do	" 16th	do front line shelled	W.R.
do	" 17th	Relieved by 5th Kings. Two platoons left in support of ORCHARD FARM. One Company and a half went to LE PREOL, remaining two and Headquarters to BETHUNE (Ecole at Jeanes Fuller)	W.R.
BETHUNE			
do	do 18th	Working parties from LE PREOL	W.R.
do	do 19th	Sub A & B Companies from BETHUNE changed places with C & D at LE PREOL	W.R.
do	" 20"	working parties from LE PREOL	W.R.
GIVENCHY	⎰ 21st	Relieve 5th Kings in B.1. sector. C & D Coys in front line, A & B in support. 2/Lieut Pitchforn slightly wounded	W.R.

W.R. Watson Capt.
a/ADJT. 7TH BN THE KING'S (L'POOL) REGT.

Sheet 3.

WAR DIARY
or
INTELLIGENCE SUMMARY.

(Erase heading not required.)

Army Form C. 2118

Instructions regarding War Diaries and Intelligence Summaries are contained in F.S. Regs., Part II. and the Staff Manual respectively. Title pages will be prepared in manuscript.

Hour, Date, Place		Summary of Events and Information	Remarks and references to Appendices
GIVENCHY	July 22nd	Trenches.	W.R.
do	" 23rd	do	W.R.
do	" 24th	do	W.R.
do	" 25th	Relieved. Move to LE PRÉOL 10 a.m. 4 officers and 20 NCOs att. attached to 5 Field Coy RE for training	W.R.
LE PREOL		at RORRE	
do	" 26th	7 a.m. Running drill 9.30 a.m. Company parades	W.R.
do	" 27th	Daily training	W.R.
do	" 28th	Move to VENDIN	W.R.
VENDIN			
VENDIN	" 29th	Daily training	W.R.
do	" 30th	do	W.R.
do	" 31st	do	W.R.

W Rutherford Lieut

GAFFT

a/ ADJT. 7TH BN THE KING'S (L'POOL) REGT.

6th Infantry Brigade.
2nd Division.

(Battn. attached 21st
Bde. 7th Div. 28.8.15)

WAR DIARY

1/7th BATTN. THE KING'S (LIVERPOOL) REGIMENT.

A U G U S T

1 9 1 5

WAR DIARY
or
INTELLIGENCE SUMMARY.

(Erase heading not required.)

Army Form C. 2118

Hour, Date, Place	Summary of Events and Information	Remarks and references to Appendices
1st Aug 1915 VENDIN-LEZ-BETHUNE	Church Parade. Swimming at Baths, BETHUNE. Regimental sports in the afternoon.	
2nd Aug 15	Company Parades. B Company working with R.E.	
3rd Aug 15 Essars	Battalion Paraded temporarily from the 6th Bde for instruction purposes. Work with the 2nd Division. R.E. proceeded to Supts in ESSARS.	
4th Aug 15 ESSARS	Working Parties with R.E. at CAMBRIN GIVENCHY	
5th Aug 15	— do — Officer instruction class in Bomb work at GORRE	
6th Aug 15	— do —	
7th Aug 15	— do —	
8th Aug 15	N & I Working party started. 7 men wounded. Church Parade. Battalion Instruction Parade by the Company Officers. Bathing Parades; letter Competition. Service held out to the Battalion. This letter was from the G.O.C. of the 6th Bde on the occasion of the Battalion leaving the Brigade.	
9th Aug 15	Working Parties at PONT FIXE, WINDY CORNER and CAMBRIN. Thunder storm at 9.30 am & 2.30 pm. 9/16 + many casualties. Officers attend class at GORRE.	
10th Aug 15	Working Parties as above also officer class	
11th Aug 15	— do —	
12th Aug 15	— do —	

Army Form C. 2118.

WAR DIARY
or
INTELLIGENCE SUMMARY.
(Erase heading not required.)

Instructions regarding War Diaries and Intelligence
Summaries are contained in F. S. Regs., Part II.
and the Staff Manual respectively. Title pages
will be prepared in manuscript.

Hour, Date, Place	Summary of Events and Information	Remarks and references to Appendices
13 Aug.15 ESSARS.	Working Parties, Officers attend R.E. Class at GORE. Warning parties at PONTFIXE area to feel the frontline trenches preparatory for the keep.	
14 Aug.15	Working parties no change.	
15 Aug.15	Church Parade. Battn. Sgts. Major in the afternoon	
16 Aug.15	Working parties as for 13th.	
17 Aug.15	" " " 13th	
18 Aug.15	" " " 13th. Two Germans	
	deserters came over BETHUNE at 7pm to	
19 Aug.15	Aeroplane flew over BETHUNE no machine change	
20 Aug.15	Working parties as for 13th.	
21 Aug.15	" " " 13th. PONTFIXE working party in ESSARS for water end?	
22 Aug.15	party returns to billets in 13th. Church Parade and the Transport got a Bath Cricket Match A/B v C/D in the afternoon C/D won	
23 Aug.15	Working parties as for 13th.	
24 Aug.15	" " Junior Officers 13th. County Officer instructs	
25 Aug.15	Working parties as for the 13th. Lieut. J.E. TOONE 2nd Regt. N.York Regt. joined and took over the Duties of Assistant.	

III Sheet.

WAR DIARY
or
INTELLIGENCE SUMMARY.

Army Form C. 2118

(Erase heading not required.)

Instructions regarding War Diaries and Intelligence Summaries are contained in F.S. Regs., Part II. and the Staff Manual respectively. Title pages will be prepared in manuscript.

Hour, Date, Place	Summary of Events and Information	Remarks and references to Appendices
26 Augt.15. ESSARS	Working parties as for 15th. Instructions of Gunner Officer by the C.O.	
27 Augt.15 —	Working parties as for 13th. Instructions of Gunner Officer by 2nd in Command	
28 Augt.15 —	Working parties as for 13th. The Battalion moved out of Billets at ESSARS into Bivouac near the junction of the LA-BASSEE–PREOL Canal and attached to the Brigade for working parties.	
29 Augt.15 Bivouac	Working parties at PONTINE, The KEEP, SIDDURY etc with the R.E. Weather very wet.	
30 Augt.15 —	Working parties as for the 29th Instant.	
31 Augt.15 —	Working parties as for the 29th Instant.	

G. Loyne Knight Capt.
For Lt Col The Buffs (E. Kent Regt)

2ND DIVISION
5TH INFY BDE

1-7TH BATTALION
   THE KING'S (LIVERPOOL REGT)
      SEP - NOV 1915

Box 2784

5th Infantry Brigade.
2nd Division.

Battn. joined Bde. 4.9.15.

1/7th BATTN. THE KING'S (LIVERPOOL REGIMENT).

SEPTEMBER

1915

Army Form C. 2118.

WAR DIARY
or
INTELLIGENCE SUMMARY.
(Erase heading not required.)

Instructions regarding War Diaries and Intelligence Summaries are contained in F. S. Regs., Part II. and the Staff Manual respectively. Title pages will be prepared in manuscript.

Hour, Date, Place	Summary of Events and Information	Remarks and references to Appendices
1915		
1st September BIVOUACS	Garrison PONT FIXE. Working Parties at Cannan Farm and SIDBURY.	F.G.T.
2nd "	Working Parties as above with additional 100 OR & 3 Officers on night Working Party. Conroy Officers attended RE. Conference at 10 AM. Battalion moved from Bivouac to Billets in ESSARS.	F.G.T.
3rd ESSARS.	Mining shifts at Orchard mine, Red House, White House sunk Rd and Duck's Bill mine 105 NCOs men attached to 176 Coy RE for mining purposes. Working Party at Tilbury. 9 men rejoined from hospl.	F.G.T.
4th "	Working parties as for 3rd Instant. Orders at PONT FIXE received by 6 o'clock.	F.G.T.
5th "	Working parties as for 3rd Instant.	F.G.T.
6th "	Working Parties " " " "	F.G.T.
7th "	Working Parties " " " " Draft of 76 men arrived and inspected by GO in the afternoon. CO attended conference at 5.2 Brigade.	F.G.T.
8th "	Working parties as for 3rd Instant.	F.G.T.
9th "	Working " " " "	F.G.T.

2nd Sheet.

Army Form C. 2118.

WAR DIARY
or
INTELLIGENCE SUMMARY.
(Erase heading not required.)

Instructions regarding War Diaries and Intelligence Summaries are contained in F.S. Regs., Part II. and the Staff Manual respectively. Title pages will be prepared in manuscript.

Hour, Date, Place	Summary of Events and Information	Remarks and references to Appendices
10th Sept 1915 ESSARS.	Working parties as for the 3rd Instant	J.T.
11th	Working parties ———— Pte. Lylegon gazetted to commission in the 3/7 Kings & left for England. Capt. Hewett & 2/Lt. Hedden proceeded on leave.	J.T.
12th	Working parties as for the 3rd Instant.	J.T.
13th	Working parties as ———— all working parties & mining shifts relieved in the evening. Found Escorts for parties on LE TOURET, ESSARS LINE, and Central Post at GORRE	J.T.
14th	Battalion at Rest. Men cleaning up, Interviews known by Coys, Bathing parades & changing underclothing.	J.T.
15th	Running Drill. Close order drill and arm drill and general setting up drill.	J.T.
16th	Running, Battalion Gymkhana. In the afternoon Mining shifts resumed as per 3rd Instant; also 100 men attached to 176 Coy R.E. at GORRE.	J.T.
17th	Usual working parties as for 3rd Inst. also additional working parties at MOAT FARM & PONT FIXE	J.T.

2nd Sheet.

Army Form C. 2118.

WAR DIARY
or
INTELLIGENCE SUMMARY.
(Erase heading not required.)

Instructions regarding War Diaries and Intelligence
Summaries are contained in F.S. Regs., Part II.
and the Staff Manual respectively. Title pages
will be prepared in manuscript.

Hour, Date, Place	Summary of Events and Information	Remarks and references to Appendices
18th Sept 15. ESSARS.	Usual working parties to Rly Dump. Control Post of 9 RRF relieved, the other Posts still found by Battalion.	Lt.
19th Sept 15. ESSARS.	Usual working parties as for 3rd Inst also additional parties to MOAT HOUSE, LAVENDER LANE SIDINGS and Caterin Farm	Lt.
20th Sept 15 ESSARS.	Usual mining parties furnished, men allotted to 5oba R.S. GORRE relieved to 50ba R.S.	Lt.
21st Sept 15. —	Working parties in trenches. Conference at 5 Bde H.Q. Co' Canspb.	Lt.
22nd Sept 15. —	Working Parties.	Lt.
23rd Sept 15. —	Working Parties.	Lt.
24th Sept 15 TRENCHES	Battalion proceeded to take up position in Trenches and relieved working parties detached to various Battalions of the Brigade	Lt.

4th Bucks

Army Form C. 2118.

WAR DIARY
or
INTELLIGENCE SUMMARY.
(Erase heading not required.)

Instructions regarding War Diaries and Intelligence Summaries are contained in F.S. Regs., Part II. and the Staff Manual respectively. Title pages will be prepared in manuscript.

Hour, Date, Place	Summary of Events and Information	Remarks and references to Appendices
25th Sept/15. TRENCHES. 4 ESSARS	The Battalion took part in the operation of the 5th Batt. covering the left flank of the Battalion and finding several working parties connected with the operation. Lt. Paterson wounded with staff of Hankow & killed 2 missing 13 Wounded. The Battalion was withdrawn to Billets in ESSARS late at night.	JCI
26th Sept/15. ESSARS.	Day spent in cleaning up etc.	JCI
27th Sept/15. ESSARS & TRENCHES	Battalion relieved Glasgow Highlanders in B.I. in the Trenches. Lt. Redding accidentally wounded coming in from patrol. T. Capt. Clarke ordered to join 1/9 Kings Liverpool Regt.	JCI
28th Sept/15. TRENCHES & ESSARS.	Battalion relieved at 8.20 p.m. from Trenches by 1/1 Bucks. Cavalliero during the day. 1 man killed 3 wounded. Regt. to ESSARS late at night.	JCI
29th Sept. ESSARS	A and C Coys proceeded to Trenches I.E. Church at Cambrin to be in support Queens Regt and Glasgow Highlanders. Cleared up Billets to make Room for Oxford & Bucks Light Infantry.	JCI

(73989) W4141—463. 400,000. 9/14. H.&J.Ltd. Forms/C. 2118/10.

5 Sheets

WAR DIARY
or
INTELLIGENCE SUMMARY.

Army Form C. 2118.

Hour, Date, Place	Summary of Events and Information	Remarks and references to Appendices
30th Sept 15 ESSARS	2 Companies from Trenches 2 in Ets. draft in :-	

[signature]
Capt
ADJT. 7TH BN THE KING'S (L'POOL) REGT.

5th Infantry Brigade.
2nd Division.

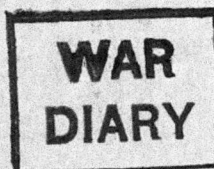

1/7th BATTN. THE KING'S (LIVERPOOL REGIMENT).

OCTOBER

1 9 1 5

Sheet I

Army Form C. 2118.

WAR DIARY
or
INTELLIGENCE SUMMARY.
(Erase heading not required.)

Instructions regarding War Diaries and Intelligence Summaries are contained in F.S. Regs., Part II. and the Staff Manual respectively. Title pages will be prepared in manuscript.

Place	Hour, Date	Summary of Events and Information	Remarks and references to Appendices
ESSARS	Oct 1st 1915	The Battalion left ESSARS at 2 p.m. for rendezvous of 5th Bgde near VERMELLES. After dusk took up position in	W.R.
VERMELLES		LANCASHIRE TRENCH, a reserve trench in front of VERMELLES. Found working parties for front line	W.R.
do	Oct 2nd	Working parties, carrying & burying parties by day & night.	W.R.
do	Oct 3rd	Left trenches at 11 a.m. and moved to BETHUNE. 3 W.O. wounded among them at 2 p.m. Casualties 9 of which included 2 accidental	W.R.
BÉTHUNE.			
do	Oct 4th	Company refitting	W.R.
ESSARS	Oct 5th	Move to ESSARS at 4 p.m.	W.R.
do	Oct 6th	Coys under Coy officers. Close order & rifle drill, organising bombing parties & rapid loading & aiming	W.R.
do	Oct 7th	do on 6th	W.R.
do	Oct 8th	Coys under Coy officers. Bombing assaults & bombing along trenches	W.R.

Sheet 21

Army Form C. 2118.

WAR DIARY
or
INTELLIGENCE SUMMARY.
(Erase heading not required.)

Hour, Date, Place		Summary of Events and Information	Remarks and references to Appendices
ESSARS	6 & 9th	Bombing demonstration.	W.R.
do	do	Left ESSARS & billeted NE of FOSSE 9, ANNEQUIN,	W.R.
ANNEQUIN	6 Oct 10th	arriving about 4 pm. Brigade reserve.	W.R.
ANNEQUIN	" 11th	Coys under Coy arrangements	W.R.
"	" 12th	Coy officers scout QUARRY & SIMS KEEP. Carrying parties out.	W.R.
"	" 13th	Working parties and carrying parties.	W.R.
"	" 14th	Working parties by day & night	W.R.
"	" 15th	do do	W.R.
"	" 16th	do do	W.R.
"	" 17th	do do	W.R.
"	" 18th	Working party of 400 men by day	W.R.
"	" 19th	do	W.R.
"	" 20th	do	W.R.
ANNEZIN	" 21st	Working party 400 men. At 2.30 pm move to ANNEZIN	W.R.
		arrive 5 pm.	
ANNEZIN	" 22nd	Running drill, adjutants parade, Company training.	W.R.
"	" 23rd	Morning as 22nd. Route march in afternoon	W.R.

Sheet 3.

Army Form C. 2118.

WAR DIARY
or
INTELLIGENCE SUMMARY.

(Erase heading not required.)

Instructions regarding War Diaries and Intelligence Summaries are contained in F.S. Regs., Part II. and the Staff Manual respectively. Title pages will be prepared in manuscript.

Hour, Date, Place		Summary of Events and Information	Remarks and references to Appendices
ANNEZIN	Oct 24th	Baths for men College des Jeunes filles. BETHUNE	W.R.
do	" 25th	Raining all day. Company inspections & lectures.	W.R.
do	" 26th	Company training & bombing practice. Route march.	W.R.
do	" 27th	as 26th	W.R.
do	" 28th	Rain. Parade 9.30 – 11 am. Lectures in billets.	W.R.
do BEUVRY	" 29th	Capt Pinkham 2/Lt Hopkins 8 NCOs & 110 men attached to 180th MINING COY. R.E. Battalion moved to BEUVRY at 1 pm.	W.R.
BEUVRY	" 30th	Trench cleaning & digging parties out. 1 NCO 16 men	W.R.
do	" 31st	do 60	W.R.
		attached to 251st Coy. R.E.	

W Rutherford Lieut
o/a a/Capt 4th Kings (L'pool Regt.)

5th Infantry Brigade.

2nd Division.

(Battn. transferred to
22nd Bde. 7th Div.
11.11.15)

WAR DIARY

1/7th BATTN. THE KING'S (LIVERPOOL REGIMENT).

NOVEMBER

1 9 1 5

Army Form C. 2118.

7 BATTALION KING'S LIVERPOOL REGIMENT.

WAR DIARY
or
INTELLIGENCE SUMMARY.

(Erase heading not required.)

Hour, Date, Place		Summary of Events and Information	Remarks and references to Appendices
1-11-15	BEUVRY	Usual Working Parties. C of E. Church parade	
2-11-15	—	Usual Working Parties	
3"	—	Usual Working Parties. Draft from England of 56 men & 9 men rejoined from hospital.	
4"	—	Working Parties for Trenches	
5"	BETHUNE	Moved Billets to MONTMORENCY Bks	
6"	—	Working parties of 300 men to Cambrin	
7"	—	" "	
8"	—	" "	
9"	—	Bn. Hdqrs employed as Bde	
10"	—		
11"	LE PREOL	Companies employed near Coy Officers. Bn. moved Billets to Le Preol. Working parties of 400 men for trenches. Retained temporarily No 27/5-Bde	
12"	BETHUNE TRENCHES	HdQtrs and B H. Coys to Trenches. B.I. took over from B Moved to Billets in FERNIE - Dv. R.O.I. Bethune Trenches waterlogged	
13"	—	Quiet day in Trenches. Trench Mortar proved a boon to everyone	

Army Form C. 2118.

WAR DIARY
or
INTELLIGENCE SUMMARY.
(Erase heading not required.)

Instructions regarding War Diaries and Intelligence Summaries are contained in F.S. Regs., Part II. and the Staff Manual respectively. Title pages will be prepared in manuscript.

Hour, Date, Place	Summary of Events and Information	Remarks and references to Appendices
BETHUNE & TRENCHES 14th Nov 15	B.H.C. Coys returned by A + D Coys former returned to Billets in Bethune. 2573 Pte William A. Coy killed night 14/15 by a sniper 2574 Pte Denton A " wounded by same bullet - no phisitions and afterwards died of same wound	ff. ff. ff.
15th	nothing unusual	ff.
16th	A + D Coy relieved by B.H. Coy 2nd Dn in the trenches	ff. ff./7
17th	Ordinary Trench routine. Wiring party out	ff./7
18th	B.H. Coy relieved by A + D Coys in trenches	ff./7
19th	nothing unusual	
20th	A + D Coys relieved by B + C Coys. R.H.Q. shelled with 8" ammunition piercing shells for about 4 hours. One man slightly wounded.	ff.
21st	Usual Trench Routine. A Coy took over a further piece of Trench from 1/4 Cameron.	ff.
22nd	Bethune. Relieved from trenches by 2nd Worcester's. Held ff. Battalion proceeded to Billets in FERME - DU ROI. BETHUNE.	ff.

WAR DIARY or INTELLIGENCE SUMMARY

Army Form C. 2118

3 Mtd [?]

Instructions regarding War Diaries and Intelligence Summaries are contained in F.S. Regs., Part II. and the Staff Manual respectively. Title Pages will be prepared in manuscript.

(Erase heading not required.)

Place	Date	Hour	Summary of Events and Information	Remarks and references to Appendices
BETHUNE	23.4.15	—	Company Parades and working parties.	F.L.
"	24.4.15	—	A & B Coy proceeded to Le QUESNOY for duty as working parties. H.Q. Co. C & D Coy proceeded to the old factory Bethune.	F.L.
"	25.4.15	—	H.Q. Co. C & D Coy moved Billets to LE CHOQUAUT	F.L.
LE CHOQUAUT	26.4.15	—	Bathing parade for C & D Coy. Afterwards Coys near Coy Officers.	F.L.
"	27.4.15	—	H.Q. Coy (A & B Coy from Le QUESNOY) to Billets in BETHUNE. C & D Coys Coys and W. Gunners & Le QUESNOY for working parties	F.L.
BETHUNE	28.4.15	—	Sunday. Rest day except working parties.	F.L.
"	29.4.15	—	A & B Coy Rest - Bath. Afterwards Inspection of Kit etc. 150 men went in Buses to Divisig Games for working parties at 4.30 p.m.	F.L.
"	30.4.15	—	Working parties only. Red. orders for Bn to be permanently transferred to the 7th Div. from 1st May providentive.	F.L.

Rasavou[?]
Lt. Colonel
Comdg 4 Bn. King's(Liverpool) Regt.

SUBJECT.

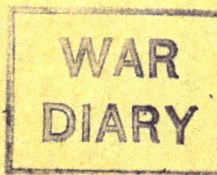

7TH DIV.

No.	Contents.	Date.
	22ND INF. BDE. — 1/7 BATT'N, The KING'S REGIMENT. (The LIVERPOOLS) — DEC, 1915	

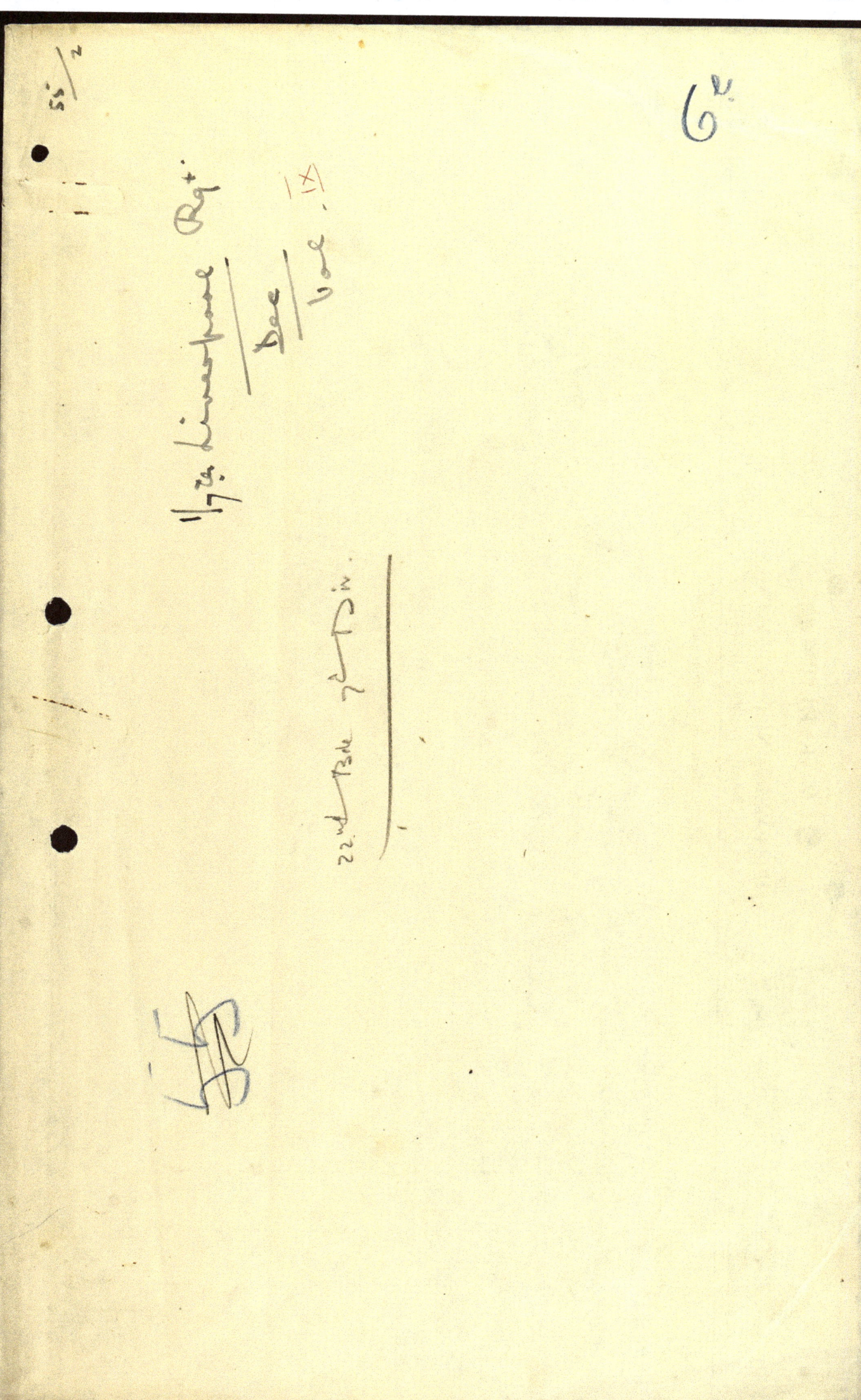

Army Form C. 2118

WAR DIARY or INTELLIGENCE SUMMARY

(Erase heading not required.)

7th Bn. King's (Pool) Regt — Decr 1915

Place	Date	Hour	Summary of Events and Information	Remarks and references to Appendices
BETHUNE	Dec 1st		Coys under Coy officers	
"	2nd		Inspection of Battalion by Cmdy Officer	
"	3rd		Inspection by G.O.C. 2nd Div. who said Good-bye on the Bn joining 7th Div.	
"	4th		Battalion marched from BETHUNE to FONTES-ST-HILAIRE, and attached to the 22nd Brigade.	
FONTES ST HILAIRE	5th		Battalion entrained at LILLERS at 10.21 pm to go to SALEUX near AMIENS and arrived there at 11.45 am	
BRIQUEMESNIL	6th		Left Railway station at SALEUX and marched to billets in BRIQUEMESNIL	
"	7th		Battalion cleaning up their Billets	
"	8th		" " and also the village	
"	9th		Coys under Coy officers. Capt. T. Major SE Harriott gazetted T.Lt.Colonel off 6-11-15. Authy known Gazette dy. 7-12-15.	
"	10th		Coys under Coy officers and Route march.	
"	11th		Coys in Billets, very wet day.	
"	12th		Church parade.	
"	13th		Coy and Battalion parades. Regtl Concert Room opened.	
"	14th		Coy and Battalion Parades.	
"	15th		" " " Lieut. Humphreys rejoined from England.	

Army Form C. 2118

WAR DIARY
or
INTELLIGENCE SUMMARY
(Erase heading not required.) 7th Kings (Pool) Regt. December 1917

2nd Sheet.

Place	Date	Hour	Summary of Events and Information	Remarks and references to Appendices
BRIQUE-MESNIL	Dec 16th		Coy & Battalion Training	
"	17th		Coy & Battalion Training	
"	18th		Battalion Route march with musical exercises.	
"	19th		Sunday. Church Parade	
"	20th		Coy and Battalion Training	
"	21st		Coy & Battalion Training	
"	22nd		Coy & Battalion Training	
"	23rd		Battalion Training	
"	24th		Brigade Training	
"	25th		Christmas Day. Church parade.	
"	26th		Sunday Church parade	
"	27th		Coy and Battalion Training	
"	28th		Battalion Training.	
WARLUS	29th		Moved billets to WARLUS.	
"	30th		Coy & Battalion Parade	
"	31st		Brigade Training	

Lt-Colonel
Comdg 7th Bn Kings (Pool) Regt.

www.ingramcontent.com/pod-product-compliance
Lightning Source LLC
Chambersburg PA
CBHW081454160426
43193CB00013B/2481